ONLY BELIEVE

Also by Jennifer Bartell:

Traveling Mercy

Only Believe

poems

JENNIFER BARTELL

THE WORD WORKS
WASHINGTON, D.C.

Acknowledgments

Thank you to the editors at the journals where some of these poems first appeared:

Aunt Chloe: A Journal of Artful Candor: "Creators," "Moonsie's House," "Possibilities," "Martha & Mary," and "Ecclesiastes 3"
The Texas Review: "And Gawd"

Thanks

To Carolyne Wright for judging and choosing this book for the Hilary Tham Capital Collection, Series Editor Brad Richard, President of The Word Works Nancy White, and all the good folks at The Word Works who had a hand in the publication of this book: thank you.

Thanks to Mariahdessa Ekere-Tallie for your bravery and sistership, especially your book *Dear Continuum: Letters to a Poet Crafting Liberation*, which has buoyed me. Thanks to Remica Bingham-Risher; your book *What We Ask of Flesh* gave me a model for some of the poems in this collection. Thank you to The Watering Hole Poetry Retreat for bringing me into fellowship with these two women. To Ray McManus for inviting me to write ekphrasis for the Write Around Series. To the editors of *The Texas Review* and *Aunt Chloe*, especially Sharan Strange. To Maya Marshall for being a steady sister. To Tara Betts for friendship and blessing me with your words. Special thanks to Ed Madden for being the first editor of this book, for the careful notes and feedback, for the undying support, for being there whenever I call.

And finally, to my husband Lester. Thank you for being my anchor, for freeing me with your love, for having my back, front, and sides always. I love you.

Contents

for the survivors

&

in memory of Irene Harvin McCray, aka "Moonsie"

I.

Oh

the *oh* of the open mouth
the *oh* of Hosanna
the *oh* of *Oh, how good is the Lord*
the *o* my mouth makes on the choir
his lips *ohing* on the row behind me
the *oh* of *Lo, he is with you always,*
even to the end of this age.
the *oh* of she got some ho-ish ways
the *oh* of holy and wholly
the *oh* of *Oh, God! You listen to his prayers too?*
the *oh* of my harrowed soul
the *oh* of let's go play hide-and-go-seek
the *oh* of what we know

my mouth makes an *o* at the frosted
bathroom window and his shadow
blocks the light

Oh, how good it is to know the Lord

Believer

Ma asks: *Did he touch you down there?*

He says he'll give me a Barbie
if I don't say anything

But I don't want a Black one
since I already hate myself

I am five years old
I peed my clothes
during naptime
I put on red overalls
and a white turtleneck
with pink elephants

I say: *No*
And then *yes*
She gives me a hug

I ask to read the Bible

Eve

I was born with gills and a razor fin,
I was born with salt water

in my mouth in the middle of a cotton field.
I didn't learn to swim until late. God kept

me from much harm. God put me in much
harm. I still got them scars from when I fell.

Folk say I got eyes like my daddy.
Folk say I walk like my daddy. I was born between

the seeds of a fig, a sticky fruit hanging low,
waiting to be devoured.

Jephthah's Daughter

My timbrels and hips are ready
for dancing.
Here comes father yonder!
He has been victorious
and I meet him midway.
He wails, for now I am the sacrifice
he promised to God.

I wail.

How merciful our God.
How merciful our fathers.

He agrees to let me go to the mountain
top to bewail my virginity
with my best girls.

For two months we stay on the mountain.

And then my father keeps
his promise to God.

I went up that mountain a virgin
but did not come down one.

They will write that I never
knew a man.

Mary of Magdala

They say I was a prostitute.
One woman who is a sinner
is about the same as another.
But I am no Mary of Bethany,
that one who dried Jesus' feet
with her hair.

I am Mary of Magdala,
meaning Tower of the Fishes.
I learned how to fish as a young
girl. Come, let me show you,
so that you may eat all
the days of your life.

There Will Always Be Jesus

I do not interview her today.
I am here at my aunt's
house on Angel Road,
Grandma Moonsie's
home now since
the car accident:
her wrists shattered
all hope of her ever
living alone again.

She has a room in the house
like the wayward child
who tried it on her own
but had to return home.
There is no Malcolm
and no Martin in her room
but plenty of Jesus,
Jesus on the cross,
Jesus in midair,
Jesus during the Last Supper.

Her stacks of Bibles
and Sunday school books
look as old as she
was fifty years ago.
A page out of a Bible,
Psalm 118, is on the floor.
Her window, facing
the setting sun, is closed
and she has the blinds
pulled up.

I lie down
on her bed
and fall asleep.
I'll awake with a quilt
draped over my legs.
The Lord is on
my side; I will
not fear: what can
man do unto me?

And Gawd

Plain glass windows with graffiti
are the stand-in-stained windows,
so stained, no light shines through,
spray paint thick like the Holy Ghost.
Jesus looks like a pimp
with smooth waves in his hair.
The artist misspelled
my granddaddy's name.
He wasn't Sunny like the sun, God of Sky,
he was Sonny like Son of God.
My Black Jesus can do anything.
Watch and see if you don't believe me.
Watch and see me like Watch Night Service
on New Year's Eve. If I close my eyes tight,
I can hear Grandaddy Sonny beating the drums
and see the altar-desk where my Ma learned
her letters, her lunch pail half empty with a biscuit
and cold fatback. Pews smell like Pledge and sweat.
I open my eyes and see myself on the front row
of one of those pews, a little girl with Mary Janes
and pig tails. I'm curled up on the front row for a nap.
Bishop is hollering into the microphone
he does not need, other hand holding his hearing aid.
And Gawd!… he booms. The head usher, my mother, wakes
me up. Later, we'll form a half circle around the altar
to take communion. Then there will be the washing
of the saints' feet. I'll go home and wonder if
what my cousin does to me makes me a sinner,
if I could reset somehow and be a virgin again.
I'll wonder if drinking the grape juice
and eating the stale wafer
would cleanse me and make me whole,
if I could ever be a saint washing—
towel girded around my waist—then drying them
precious sanctified feets.

Creators

She is sewing a quilt
in my dreams. Her salt
and pepper cornrows
have the same pattern
as the pink and black flower fabric;
her hands piece them together
with the needle and thread.
The quilt is the length
of the bed and she is almost
finished. All that is needed
is the tacking that binds
the layers. She is singing gospel
songs, remixing them as she
goes. I am at the other end
of the quilt with a pen in
my hand, my square of quilt
a notebook. I'm waiting
for the words of our story,
to tell
myself the one I am scared
to hear.

Biscuits

I step into Granny's house and smell
biscuits. They are not sitting
on the table. She does not greet
me with a smile. She is humming
over a sink full of dishes.

I still do not know how to tie
my shoes: 9 upside down
is still a 6.

Dem biscuits
she makes from scratch.
Dem biscuits
a little dark on top.
Dem biscuits
fluffy in the middle.
Dem biscuits
that were so warm you
could feel and see the steam coming
off them when you broke them open.

I like mine with butter and grape jelly—
I am learning how to take the sweet
with the salty, the cool with the warm.

He is in his bedroom pretending
to do homework. He will come out
eventually to ask me to play a game
of hide-and-go-seek.

I will not say no.
I will not say stop.

A pail full of old rags
is burning on the back
porch to keep the gnats
away. Granny starts singing
a different gospel song. I listen.

I wait
for my Ma to finish sewing panties
and come take me home.

Polaroid: Cake at Moonsie's

I am a menace
                over the cake,
smiling.
The whites of my eyes masked
under thick eyelashes. Just where
the Polaroid frame cuts my head off:
black little curls come down my forehead.
A white turtleneck, hands
crossed and propped on Moonsie's table.

The two-layer
baby pink cake
with white frosting in cursive writing
will not say whose birthday it is.
The white frosting trim lines
the sides, a red rose with
two green leaves sit on top.

Moonsie's table, where she sews, where
she spreads butter and jelly onto biscuits,
wood-grained plastic, pale, almost green.
Her table is where he ate.
On her table is the cake, with one dark pink,
unlit candle; a set of keys with a fuchsia key chain
sits close to the cake.
I watch them.

The Polaroid's surface is shiny but little scratches
and fingerprints taint the cake and me
and the woman and the table and the keys.
The white plastic frames it.
There. Where it is supposed to say
who the cake is for and the day.

But that don't make no never mind.
We are at Moonsie's house…
her old, white house in Muddy Creek.
Her house that is surrounded by woods
on one side and by corn fields on the other.
Her house down a dusty, dirt lane,
her house where the porch is made of wooden planks,
her house the snakes lived under,
where her bathroom is his favorite room.

In the bathroom,
I lift up my white turtleneck
and drop my pants to the floor.
He wants me to remain silent,
he wants to give me Barbie dolls.

A hand is pushing my left shoulder,
though the picture shows no movement,
I can feel it.
This woman beside me with a
white buttoned-down sweater
and black, floral dress, maybe my mother,
maybe an auntie.
The table cuts from her thighs down
and the top of the picture
cuts off the rest of her body.

Alzheimer's: Pound Cake Anxiety

The Young and The Restless came on.
You closed the oven door to bake.
Your mind nervous. It cannot fall.
We were on the porch, jumping around
like mixing spoons. All-purpose flour
is strong and holds the cake. Your floors
were weak; the flour was wrong.
Your swollen time won't stand over ovens
ever again. No kitchen will feel your patience.
Away from afternoons that lasted too long
and cakes that flopped when purpose failed:
Y'all made my cake fall.

Blackberries

My cousins and I scrapped for blackberries in
the summer. Our noses trained to the

juice in each pearly, purple bulb. When
we found them the palms of our hands

were stained with their blood,
our forearms streaked with bloody lines.

We cradled them in our upturned
shirts 'til we got back to the wooden planks

of Moonsie's porch. And these were not sweet
enough for our restless tongues. In a white

bowl our blackberries went and we sprinkled them with sugar.

The blackberry enveloped in white. In this we delight:

The blackberry's juice now sweeter.
We say to the blackberries: *You are not enough.*

Born Again: A Prayer

Middle school cafeteria
Girls talk about who's a virgin and who's not

Can I be a virgin again? Or am I still a virgin? I didn't have a choice. ~~I didn't know what I was doing.~~ I didn't know what was being done to me. I was just a little girl. Those times don't count…do they? Please say that I am a virgin. Can I be a born-again virgin like I was a born-again Christian? Do You hear the prayers of girls whose virginity was stolen from them? Cover me in Your blood. Wash me in Your blood. Make me whole. ~~Wash this sin away.~~

The Window

The window was frosted, like my thoughts,
always a veil, blurring the image of the other
side, not as clear as it should be or rather like
my memory of how many times it happened—
exactly, which makes me question if it happened
at all. But where does a child conjure such violence
against her own body?

The grunts, the shushing.

No eyes could penetrate this frost.
Maybe I did
not suck my thumb in the womb.
Maybe there was comfort in controlling
what went into my own mouth, like frosted flakes
with two percent milk, since Ma worried so about
the fat in whole milk.

However many times it may have happened,

the window stands not as portal,
but as mirror, an offering:
I'll hold this secret for you, too. I'll stand
between you and the world.
No one has to know.

The Interview: We Had It Hard

We used to play all the time
and make mud pies when I was little.
I learned to plait on a grass dolly.
We used to wash it hair too.
We used to have a good time playing.
I went to school at Battery Park.
It was a rotten-down two-story building.
We had one book with a green back on it.
I wore old shoes to school.
I didn't talk much as a girl.

I stopped going to school in the 6th grade.
Sometimes I would go one day to school
but when April come and tobacco come,
I didn't go to school none. When I was little
we would help the White folks sweep up the yard,
pick up the sticks and we would get a piece
of hogmeat, rice or flour for pay. They would give
us clothes sometimes, good clothes.

My ma would make
our clothes but one day I say,
"Ma, let me make my own dress." And I did.
I been sewing ever since I was big.
I was sewing with two fingers
and I have holes in my fingers
and black spots right now from that.
My ma learn me how to quilt.
I only gave my quilts away, never sold 'em.
I give them away to my family and my kin folk.
But I tell you who could make a quilt: My ma.
We used to sleep on the quilts on the floor.
We cover with the quilts—we had a time, hear?

I been cooking ever since I was big
enough to cook. I learn myself to cook.
The first thing I cook was flourbread.
"Moonsie can cook," is what my sisters
say. My sisters started calling me Moonsie
but I don't know who learn them that.
We used to make brooms out of straw
and sell them to folks for 25 cents.

These two little legs here
were the only way we used to get around.
We used to be so tired.
We had it hard, hear?
But I made it through, thank God
for that. Mama always kept clothes
and decent shoes on us.
Some people ain' had no shoe
and went barefoot. Sometimes we had grits
and peas and fried meat for breakfast.
For dinner we had rice and peas.
Daddy would buy meat.

Alzheimer's: The Lunch Pail

A handkerchief is at the bottom
of my pail,
it's a bed for the
fatback and biscuit lunch
I tote on my walk to school,
school that came Sunday was church,
a pot belly stove
in the middle of the room.
I can't wait to huddle in the pews
to get closer
to the heat—
I wonder how this heat
might be like the sulfur
and brimstone of hell,
which is where Mama says
I belong.

The cotton done
came in 'cause of the quick
work of my tiny fingers.
Harvest means no school.
Harvest means nothing but work,
but today....

Today looks like the bottom
of my lunch pail—cool
pale steely blue,
an outline.

I know my letters good
but I'm dark like the dirt,
gon' be low all my life
like it too if Mama's words
are truth.

There's something else
over there, out there beyond
the sun. When I take my eyes
like this and squint, I see it,
but it don't seem to see me yet.

Cooter Nuggets

Gone and fetch a bucket!
We cock our ears across the yard.
No one understands her toothless mouth.
We watch from the porch—
a turtle the size of a tire crosses the road,
passes in front of the paused car
that she is seated in.
Cousin cuts across the field, dust flaps
his calves. Comes back, cutting in the house,
clutches a white bucket. Makes dust tracks.
The turtle slips in the woods, into a soft swamp.
Y'all good for nothing.
Her mouth fixed for some

cooter nuggets.

Stomps in the kitchen, curses our lackadaisical-ness,
cooing about cooter meat.
Presenting: her careless grandchildren.
We jump from the porch, our mouths fixed
for blackberries.
We fight briar patches: thorns scratch our arms
Juice drips down our lips, ripe with joy.

There is simplicity and joy in the arc
of a turtle's back. Who knew
this more than her.

Sonny's Rifle

All my granddaddies died before I was born.
Maybe if they were living, they could protect me.

It hangs over Moonsie's mantle,
belonged to granddaddy Sonny.
His oily fingerprints now dust.
It is loaded, or not,
with its silent, wooden handle.

Maybe it is not on the mantle,
but on the door frame just opposite
the bathroom.

I dreamt about holding it in my hands.

Sonny used it to hunt down deer
that trampled his tomatoes,
or maybe he shot the squirrels down out of the oak trees.

It is the last thing granny
owns that once belonged to him.

It is not loaded. It is not even in my hands.
It is not even in the place where
the brain sends information it wants to forget.
And yet I remember.

I imagine it in my hands
as I'm in the bathroom with my cousin.
I point it at him like I see them do in
them Westerns Da watches.

Possibilities

The mudpies are in the sun,
the drying out and crumbling to come.
I stare up at the sky, at the Goodyear
Blimp and wonder where they are going,
where they came from. The sky is
so clear and blue, the blimp is a shiny
fish flickering in the sky.
I need to stay outside as long as possible,
wander up the dirt lane and look down the road
Left. Right. Left.
I know what's coming behind me, but in front
is the wide-open road and options forever.
I look back up at the Blimp. I want to go somewhere,
anywhere where nobody knows me.

Black Madonna

Were you a virgin even after you had Jesus? The Bible mentions Jesus' brothers—did you have those children after Jesus or were those Joseph's kids from his first marriage? Does being the Virgin Mary mean you were a virgin when you conceived Christ or does it mean you were a virgin even afterwards: all the days of your life?

Mary: Nunya.

Moonsie & Me

God is at Moonsie's knee:
She sewed on the big black
Singer sewing machine
with the gold lettering
and foot pedals. I played
with the scraps at her feet.

She knew I was a creator
even before I was born.
Let me learn you to sew.

God is a woman
on a big black Singer
sewing machine
with gold lettering.

How many times I threaded
the needle for her, still hear
the rhythm of the needle
piercing cloth, her foot
marking time on the pedal.

This is how she teaches
her future to love the past:

With needle and cloth
dirt and rain
tobacco and blackberries.
With nothing but hands
full of holes from a lifetime
of needles poking
into skin.

The needle feels like a pencil
in my hand. What will I write
with this thread today?

Even in Your Darkest Hour

I awake to her humming,
her hemming is done,
the light too low
for her to sew.

I awake to my remembering.
My eyes trying to adjust
to being back on this side.

Gawd will cover you.
Even in your darkest
hours. He will
be your refuge.
Lean on him.

You all right, honey?
I think no,
but say yes, ma'am.
I am here with her
but back at the house
in Muddy Creek too.

I will never have the words
to tell her what happened.
She will never have the words
to tell me what happened
when she was thirteen
and had a son.

I will not know the right questions
to ask. But will write what I know.

Hope

my mouth mends

what my flesh becomes

sew that patch back

hem your tongue

we all have our

crosses to bear

II.

Moonsie's House

The mirages in the road disappear
as I get closer.
The cotton ain't high; it ain't even cotton yet,
the flower just starting to come on the bush.
A man steps out shirtless on his porch,
a slice of watermelon in his hand,
sunset rays drenched on his glistening skin.
The bean fields are an ocean:
one farmer has pole propped t-shirts
like scarecrows in his field, so as to trick the deer,
who wander the fields and woods at dusk for dinner.
A stop sign is in front of me and to the right
the red sign says Do not Enter.
I go straight… it is the way home, where
I am not headed

through small country towns with no
stop lights and a city named for a lake
that's gone or that maybe never existed.
I stop at Young's Convenience Store
for Cajun boiled peanuts, their briny memory
in my mouth even after the Cherry Pepsi
chaser. These roads lead towards home,
but the compass inside of me says to go
to the spot in the woods where Moonsie's white
house once was; the fields done took it over.
I can still see the outline of the dirt lane…

Moonsie would babysit us, my brothers
and cousins, during the summer.
And that's when it happened most often.
Hide-and-go-seek and a surprise shit
and then an undressing and a dick.
My cocoon of silence was a prison,
solitary confinement was constant.

Maybe this was the biggest sin
I committed against myself.
Maybe my screams couldn't shatter a thing
but my own mind. Maybe if I could speak clearly
and not worry about saying words right,
if I could use these words I write as witness,
if I could tell my mama sooner than when I did,
maybe things could be different.

And don't tell
me how God has a plan…or how I should never
wear pants to church. All of my life I thought
that was Moonsie's house, but she was a renter
and the White man who owned it came along
one day and told her she had to leave.

Nothing we ever have ever truly belongs to us.

The Pocketbook Lesson

Don't put your pocketbook on the floor.
Do and you won't ever have money.
Moonsie knew who not to waste her wisdom on.
Handpicked which grand-girl would inherit her knowledge.
Instead of setting her pocketbook down, she put it in her lap
whenever she was anywhere else in the world but her own home.
At the table, about to eat: *Gal, run wet up a wash rag for me.*
She would use the damp cloth and wipe her hands good.
Now she was ready to eat.
Moonsie didn't put no napkin in her lap, the pocketbook
was already there. She would eat her fried chicken and rice,
her toothless mouth somehow making do. Drink a full glass
of water. Then put that pocketbook on her shoulder,
without really saying she was ready to go, 'cause she wasn't.
She was just securing the bag before it was a trend to secure
the bag. And it wasn't a purse. That's how you could shape
your mouth sometimes, that wasn't the place where you stored
your mints, strawberry hard candy, and your handkerchiefs
and that bill you needed to go uptown to pay tomorrow,
a Band-Aid or two and a Charleston Chew, a small pouch of
coins, and a bit of cash—never checks. Keep
your pocketbook…always be able to lay your eyes and hands on it.
Never sew new cloth with old cloth. Don't let your bad grandchildren
walk around the house while you trying to bake a pound cake.
And at the end when it's time to go, you won't need to
go get your pocketbook because it was with you the whole time.

Alzheimer's: The Everlasting Arm

her granddaughter
stands
at the edge of
a cornfield

she hasn't been
born

yet

she will
tote her story
one day

Well Made

"A well-made body lasts a long time."
—Lea, in Colette's *Cheri*

Thick legs and wide hips,
an ass that a White woman
would pay for. Hers was grown,
born and bred in the South, brought
up on beans and rice and fried chicken
with cornbread. Legs strong from foot
races with her male cousins. She always
was the winner. Lips that they now call
beautiful and voluptuous, and a decidedly
African nose, wide to breathe in God's
air with pleasure. Teeth that ain't exactly
straight, and ain't crooked either, they're
not white, but not yellow.
Acne scars and small blemishes corrupt
her skin, her hands look like they wash
too many dishes. Her thighs strong
from the labor of holding up that ass.

She didn't have a choice. They got them
big ol' butts like that on both sides
of her family. Sometimes she wears her
hair as an afro, and others as cornrows.
Some White woman thinks she invented
box braids. Maybe a well made body
does last a long time, enough for them
to strip it down for its spare parts:
keep what they want, discard the soul,
the essence of the Blackness.
They kept Sarah Baartman's pickled vagina
in a jar for decades in France. Years before
that they paid to see her extraordinarily fat ass,
in an exhibition that was really a zoo.

Fly Brown Girls

I.

See them girls
See them girls twerk
them girls
pop

drop
      and lock
See them girls
      shake it
like a Polaroid
      picture

See that girl

          she got a donk

See this picture
is so distorted
that no one
remembers my face.

II.

Miley lifted
her pancake ass
with her big booty
Black girls as new
human zoo props.

Twerk
gets into the dictionary.
As if the word and act
had not existed
before she

dropped it like it was
lukecold
at best. The dictionary defines
twerk as
thrusting   *hip movements, low, squatting*
dance   *in a sexually provocative manner.*

This is a troublesome definition.

Iggy is a blonde
Australian in blackface
without the blackface.
The audience applauds.
But that's   not   fancy.

That's appropriation
that's been happening
since the slaveship.

Rock n' roll
could never happen
without the blues.
Jimi Hendrix
made guitars
speak in tongues.
Jazz and the blues
came from cotton fields.

And new
music is constantly
being birthed.
Or some new dance
or some old ancestral dance,
a dance that survived
                    the slaveship,
but finds new life in the blank space
of White form.

III.

This is the definition of twerking:
The beads on our cornrowed
hair keeps time against our clapping
hands and chanting mouths. We *Butterfly*
and *Tootsie Roll* on the playground
at recess,   down the block with the home-girls,
on the side of the house where Grandma couldn't see.
We girls, still nurturing the spread
of our thighs and hips, whisper
fiercely for her to *shake it girl*,
dooo now, laughing and signifying.
This is not the definition of twerking.

This is brown girls playing.
This is jump rope games and Double Dutch.
This is Miss Mary Mac dressed in black.
This is the smack of our hands when
we play patty cake or patting down
the contours of a fresh mudpie.
This is hopscotch and trading jelly shoes
or bubblegum or bracelets or a candy ring.

We brown girls switching,
swaying our not yet hips
like our aunties do,
practicing how to talk grown.

We are brown girls at play.
We are brown girl levitation.
Watch us fly.

Tell Moonsie Not to Moan

She serving the food,
big spoonfuls of pileau
dumped onto paper plates
with green beans
and sweet potato pie
or a slice of pound cake.

The line is long
and the big pot of pileau
is little, but it keeps
coming on…
the rice,
the chicken,
the sausage.

Her line is long
and it will keep coming.
She got her nose
and he got her gap
and my kitchen don't grow.
She comes back, always,
through our blood.

Martha & Mary

Mary, tell Martha to moan,
to mourn, to mend, to make.
Tell her to rip her clothes.
Tell her to sit in ashes
and never let anyone tell
her how to grieve
when you mourn
for the one you love.
Tell her that her grief made
Jesus weep, and she was
able to see the dazzling
tears of God.
Tell Martha that Lazarus
is getting up—Jesus done
spoke breath back into
his body.

Prayers

with phrases from Ross Gay's *Bringing the Shovel Down*

My trillion prayers have gone unheard.
I am a weary sheep on a forsaken field,
trying to find my way back to a place
unlike home.
Or maybe I am the wolf,
or maybe a wolf-mouthed sheep
looking for nourishment, stepping
on ground I ought not be on.

The Creek Knows How to Run

I drive through Muddy Creek to
go to my cousin's house,
which is around the corner from where
Moonsie's house once was.

Before driving up that piece of road,
I stop at the dirt lane, still visible,
a lane leading to nothing,
but growed up grass and cotton that's already
been picked.
The blackberries long gone,
leaves burnt orange.

Getting off the bus to this lane.
Going to this school because it allowed
me to go to Grandma's afterwards,
because my brothers were not old enough
to look after me yet. The time I was running
so hard I fell, slid on my bookbag and slid
back up to running in one fell swoop.

Etching out with a stick four corners
or hopscotch on the hard hearth of the yard.
Foot races with other male cousins: I always won.
Meeting here before our annual trip to Huntington
Beach State Park, where we grilled and dipped
our feet in the saltwater of the Atlantic.
Finding a chicken snake in grandma's closet.

Getting a beating for mooning cars; my brother
saying I moonwalked like Michael Jackson
as each hit of the switch slices my skin.
Granny emptying out a sack of potatoes full
of roaches and us stomping on them.
Burning rags in a pail to keep the gnats away.
Building booby traps for each other in the backyard.

Walking miles to the Lewis store for penny candy
and Little Debbie cakes and honey bun with a thick
hunk of cheese or a slice of bologna or Red Rock
and a pack of nabs or chocolate Moon Pies.
Summers listening to *The Young and The Restless* theme
song, Granny smiling at Victor Newman 'cause
he was her boyfriend.

Sitting on the wooden-planked porch,
waiting, waiting, waiting.
Taking pictures in front of the school bus
your cousin drove because back then high school
students were trusted to drive children to and
from school. Biscuits. The big, black Singer
sewing machine with gold lettering and pedals.

The best deer meat hash of my life.
Dirt bomb fights from the huge clumps
of dried out dirt in the field. Saturday morning
drop offs, watching the *Dukes of Hazzard*
and Saturday morning cartoons.

These are the memories that echo
in the brown stalks
of cotton. They play out
in front of me,
the house gliding on the air.

I love this house for what it gave me.
I hate this house for what it took from me.

I have no tears for it today.
And get into my car to drive up
that piece of road.

Hey, Jenni Lou! she greets me as she
always does. And I sit down to eat the food
she has prepared. Wait for her to give me some

Tupperware or some laundry detergent I always
need. I will get back in my car and drive back to
Columbia, crossing streams, creeks, and rivers.

Whispers

Must have been one of them fast-tailed gals. Did you see how she was dressed? She was asking for it. How old was she? Well. Doesn't matter. She shoulda known better. Why didn't she tell somebody when it happened? Why she waited twenty years before she said anything. Why didn't they call the police? Why didn't her daddy kill him? Why they always trying to tear down Black men? Don't you never be alone with *that* male relative. He didn't touch you that way; you musta have misunderstood what was happening. I don't believe her. She need Jesus. The light of God ain't in her.

The Interview: What You Came Into

It been a time when we was coming up.
I'm glad you didn't come then.

My Pa was a sharecropper. I started picking cotton
when I was 10 and doing 'bacco too.
We got paid 40 or 50 cents
to work all day long. Jesus,
I don't know how the people made it.
Stuff was cheap then.
I work so hard for 50 cents a day!
Until the sun go down. Great daddy!
I hope it never come back to dat.

We went to church every Sunday and we
walked there. People don't go all the time
now and they got something to ride in.

I would take care of myself real good.
Black and white ointment at night
and I put some cream or Vaseline on
my face in the morning. I met Sonny
when he came by the house one Sunday.
A man had told Sonny about me
and he came to see about me. He came
to the kitchen door and talked to me.
Two weeks later we went to the courthouse
in Kingstree to get married.

I felt good at the birth of my children. Aunt Blanche
helped me with all of 'em except Bobbie. Being a mom
means to me taking care of my children,
keeping them warm, putting clothes on 'em,
keeping their bellies full.

I don't remember how I felt when Sonny died in '76.
I don't remember nothing about no Civil Rights Movement.

In all I lived on the Huggins place, Roy Stuckey
place, Oddell Stuckey place, little white house
in Muddy Creek, Johnsonville projects, Lola house,
and Helen house. I was scared when I got into the car
accident in '98. I had slowly forgotten about it.
I thought I was going to die. I pray nobody
never get in a wreck.

I'm happy and glad that the Lord thought
good to spare my life. Back then folks
didn't have no time to tell us stories,
all they had time for was work. Now
everything is much better.

I'm going and you coming, honey.
You coming everyday of your life.

I want for all my grands and great grands
to go to school and get a nice education
and a good job. What can you do without
a education? You don't get too much education.
You can use something every day. If I could go to school
I woulda been a first grade teacher. Thank the old people
for what they do for you.

You don't know what you come into.

Sing

The older I
get the more
I understand
why she sang
gospel songs
all the time.

Apology

Once upon a time I thought of him
as a dark muse: source of my pain
the reason these words flow.

I don't flinch anymore at the sound
of his name. I can talk to him
without imagining him taking

his last breath with his throat
in my hands. Even at the family
cookout where I told him he

hadn't killed me, that I hadn't died.
He said he couldn't remember doing
that, but that he was sorry if he had.

If. Denial
like an invisible knife, his daughter
and granddaughter.

She Believed

After I said yes.
After she asked
me about blood.
She gave me a hug:

she believed me
she believed me
she believed me
she believed me

Ecclesiastes 3

every thing in its place
every thing in its purpose
every thing in its time
my birth leads to sure death
I am a plant that was plucked
broken and built up
weeping into my hands
and laughing at the stars
my mourning becomes dancing
I gather the stones I cast away
I embrace what time has given me
I sew my tattered clothes
my silence is over
the war inside me has stilled
it's time to speak
it's time to heal
it's time to heal
it's time to heal

Legacy

Look the eye
of the needle
in the eye
to thread it.
Don't sew
new cloth
with old cloth.

Honey, you cut
from a different
cloth.

Let me learn you how to stitch
Let me learn you how to
Let me learn you
Let me learn
Let me

This Cup

I. New Moon

All of the eggs
I will ever need
are in my ovaries
when I am born.

My mother carried
her grandson
before I was born.

II. First Quarter

These acts
have made me
a woman, years
before I should
be one. What
was done to my
body does not
match what
happens
to my mind
for years and years.

Take this cup.

III. Full Moon

Nothing but
blood again.
We know about
birthing babies
in this family.
Except me.
Still letting
myself learn
how to love.

IV. Last Quarter

They say you don't
become a woman
until your mother dies,
and I've been a woman
too soon twice now.
I know not Her will,
or if I want it to be done.

Photograph: Betty, Bobbie, & Moonsie

Aunt Betty is a bald-headed toddler held close to Moonsie.
My mother Bobbie is an infant in Moonsie's arms.

Moonsie stares at the camera unsmiling. As to say
gon' head let's be done with this; or maybe she believed

the camera would capture her soul. Moonsie shaved
all of Betty's hair off when she was a girl.

Took her into a cornfield at moonlight.
A man was there. She said, stay here.

The stalks of corn must have played cruel tricks.
She must have closed her eyes but could still see them.

Maybe that man was her daddy. Maybe my mother's
daddy was my classmate's granddaddy, but maybe

he wasn't. Maybe Moonsie regretted marrying
the man she had met just two weeks prior

on her parents' porch. She'd rather hold a grudge
than drop it. There's time for forgiveness later.

Only Believe

A church hat is a crown. A set of pews is an Amen Corner. She sits there with the other Mothers of the Church. She is waiting for the testimony portion so she can sing her song: *Only believe. Oooooh! Only believe: All things are possible if you only believe. I believe! Oooooh! I believe: All things are possible. If you only believe. Do you believe? Oooooh! Do you believe? All things are possible if you only believe.* The Holy Ghost jumped on me. There's a difference between knowing and believing. I believed because she believed. All things are possible because she did not die. If she could survive, so could I. *Do you believe? Oooooh! Do you believe? All things are possible. If you only believe.* (Repeat until you believe.)

I Believe...

all things are possible if I only believe
He didn't bring me this far to leave me
He ain't really a He/She but some entity beyond our comprehension
I am a speck in the hollow of God's hand
I am made of stardust and one day will return home
forgiveness ain't for him; it's for me
in the little girl who died in a bathroom
in the little girl resurrected but not glorified
in the woman who grew out of the corpse of that girl,
I was forced up between the thick, hard roots of Southern pine

Genesis 1:31

I wear white to her funeral.
I am one of many flower girls
who carry calla lilies to the hearse.
I am the last of her children's children.
I am her favorite grandchild,
despite how the others will dispute.
She said things to me she never told
the others. They didn't know
the questions to ask. I regret all
the questions I will not get to ask.
I do not regret her being free
of a body so wracked with arthritis
that all she could move were her eyes.
Where's Bobbie? she would ask
about my dead mother, her daughter.
She's not here, I would say instead of the truth,
not wanting to see the pain on her face anew.

At the hospital, when her heartbeat slowed
to zero, my cousin started singing
"Only Believe" and she came back to for a little while
and then she was gone. Gone like her white house.

I take on her memories:
A man comes to ask me to marry him
on my parents' porch. And I don't have many options.
I know they are ready to get rid of me, know
it's time I do something. When the preacher
says, "Now you may kiss the bride," the man will say
"Plenty time for that," and six daughters later,
thirty years later, a husband who drinks up
all the money he makes later, and I'm still
trying to figure out what it all means.

I haven't been back to that spot in the woods
where she is buried. I do not need to, she
is buried inside of me. And we visit often.
I put my head on the pillow of her soft bed,
she pulls one of her quilts over me,
I close my eyes knowing that when
I awake I will be able to see everything
that we have made. *Behold: It is good.*

Moonsie Speaks From Beyond the Grave

Don't get married. Don't have no kids.
If you have one child, you won't have no more.
You feel like you're dying. Listen.
Listen to me, girl. You are meant for more.
I been told you what you needed to do
to have a good life. A man ain't no part of it.
That ain't a man. That a dog.
I wouldn't marry him if he had gold 'round
his tail. A pregnant woman has one foot
in the graveyard. I tried to tell you,
you who were supposed to be
my change and chance,
my beginning again.
I see you made your own, your own kind of life.
I see you got married anyhow and full to the brim
with a man-child.

This is not the life I had for you.

Notes

Irene Harvin McCray aka Moonsie, January 9, 1911—June 7, 2013.

The following are ekphrasis poems written in response to art for the Write Around Series, a project by Columbia Museum of Art Writer-in-Residence Ray McManus. The poems were read at the museum on March 27, 2019:

> "Mary of Magdala" (*Christ at the Home of the Pharisee* by Artus Wolfaerts)

> "Alzheimer's: The Lunch Pail" (*A Pale Angel's Halo* by James Rosenquist)

> "Sonny's Rifle" (*Tallith for Meyer Schapiro* by Robert Motherwell)

> "The Pocketbook Lesson" (*Unidentified Portrait* by Richard Samuel Roberts)

Several poems in this collection ("Jepthah's Daughter," "Mary of Magdla," "Martha & Mary," and "Ecclesiastes 3") were inspired by Alicia Ostriker's poetry and her practice of midrash, which is described as an ancient genre that involves elaborating on Biblical stories and characters.

"Fly Brown Girls" references Nikky Finney's poem "Brown Girl Levitation" from her collection *Head Off & Split*. Phrases from these songs were used: "Hey Ya!" by Outkast, "Donk" by Soulja Boy, and "Pop, Lock, and Drop It" by Huey.

About the Author

Jennifer Bartell (Boykin) is the Poet Laureate of the City of Columbia, South Carolina. Her debut book of poetry, *Traveling Mercy*, was released in 2023. An alumna of Agnes Scott College, she is an Academy of American Poets Poet Laureate Fellow and has additional fellowships from *Callaloo* and The Watering Hole. Jennifer is an English educator and school librarian who has an MFA and an MLIS from the University of South Carolina. You can reach her online at jenniferbartellpoet.com.

About the Artist

Dogon Krigga is a Columbia, SC, multi-disciplinary artist. Krigga evolved their practice from digital art to include hand-cut paper collage and assemblage with printed and cut vinyl on acrylic and metal, as well as installations. Their work has been shown in solo and group exhibitions at venues such as Tapp's Fine Art Center, The Sumter County Gallery of Art, Columbia Museum of Art, and The Goodall Gallery. Krigga's work is found in numerous public and private collections, including the IP Stanback Museum. Krigga is a recipient of grants from the SC Arts Commission.

About The Word Works

Since its founding in 1974, The Word Works has steadily published volumes of contemporary poetry and presented public programs. Its imprints include the Washington Prize, the Tenth Gate Prize, the Hilary Tham Capital Collection, and International Editions.

Monthly, The Word Works offers free programs in its Café Muse Literary Salon. Starting in 2023, the winners of the Jacklyn Potter Young Poets Competition will be presented in the June Café Muse program.

As a 501(c)3 organization, The Word Works has received awards from the National Endowment for the Arts, the National Endowment for the Humanities, the D.C. Commission on the Arts & Humanities, the Witter Bynner Foundation, Poets & Writers, The Writer's Center, Bell Atlantic, the David G. Taft Foundation, and others, including many generous private patrons.

An archive of artistic and administrative materials in the Washington Writing Archive is housed in the George Washington University Gelman Library. The Word Works is a member of the Community of Literary Magazines and Presses.

wordworksbooks.org

Books in the Hilary Tham Capital Collection

Nathalie Anderson, *Stain*
Mel Belin, *Flesh That Was Chrysalis*
Carrie Bennett, *The Land Is a Painted Thing*
Tara Betts, *Refuse to Disappear*
Doris Brody, *Judging the Distance*
Sarah Browning, *Whiskey in the Garden of Eden*
Grace Cavalieri, *Pinecrest Rest Haven*
Nikia Chaney, *to stir &*
Cheryl Clarke, *By My Precise Haircut*
Christopher Conlon, *Gilbert and Garbo in Love*
               & *Mary Falls: Requiem for Mrs. Surratt*
Donna Denizé, *Broken Like Job*
W. Perry Epes, *Nothing Happened*
David Eye, *Seed*
Bernadette Geyer, *The Scabbard of Her Throat*
Elizabeth Gross, *this body / that lightning show*
Barbara G. S. Hagerty, *Twinzilla*
Lisa Hase-Jackson, *Flint & Fire*
James Hopkins, *Eight Pale Women*
Donald Illich, *Chance Bodies*
Brandon Johnson, *Love's Skin*
Ed Madden, *A pooka in Arkansas*
Thomas March, *Aftermath*
Marilyn McCabe, *Perpetual Motion*
Judith McCombs, *The Habit of Fire*
James McEwen, *Snake Country*
Kevin McLellan, *in other words, you/*
Miles David Moore, *The Bears of Paris*
               & *Rollercoaster*
Kathi Morrison-Taylor, *By the Nest*
M. A. Nicholson, *Around the Gate*
Tera Vale Ragan, *Reading the Ground*
Michael Shaffner, *The Good Opinion of Squirrels*
David Allen Sullivan, *Black Butterflies Over Baghdad*
Maria Terrone, *The Bodies We Were Loaned*
Hilary Tham, *Bad Names for Women* & *Counting*

Barbara Ungar, *Charlotte Brontë, You Ruined My Life*
       &   *Immortal Medusa*
Jonathan Vaile, *Blue Cowboy*
Rosemary Winslow, *Green Bodies*
Kathleen Winter, *Transformer*
Michele Wolf, *Immersion*
Joe Zealberg, *Covalence*